CW00473398

Travels of a Tin Trunk

Hidden in a corner of a musty attic I found a well travelled tin trunk, with a brass lock and leather straps. Over the passage of time, no one had thrown it out. What secrets did it hold?

Before I left Owletts, the family home in Cobham, Kent in 1994, I had become curious about the attic's dust-covered contents, but had no time to explore them. I had little idea what was there, but as the eldest son I wanted to keep alive the threads of family history. Along with cabinets, paintings and chipped china, I collected numerous family letters and photo albums, a seven-foot family tree dating back to 1760 .... and this tin trunk, and took them with me.

Owletts from the north-east

I grew up with an outline of Owletts' history and incidental family stories. The name Owletts is thought to derive from a Huguenot named Houlet, a yeoman farmer. The house was built in 1684 by Bonham Hayes and his wife Elizabeth. They placed their initials and the date on the chimneys and on the fine plaster ceiling above the stair well. Originally standing four-square, with hipped roof and casement windows, it was altered by a later Hayes who added the parapet. In 1790 it changed hands, coming to Henry Edmeades, whose daughter Maria married Thomas Baker. Thomas and Maria celebrated by creating stained-glass windows in oeil-de-boeuf windows showing their family crests, and by adding portraits in the dining room of their fathers, Henry and Samuel Baker the builder.[1] Perhaps they also replaced the casement windows with sash. One of their grandsons was Herbert Baker, my grandfather, born in 1862 the 4th son of Thomas Henry, a farmer, and his wife Frances Georgina Baker. He trained as an architect and in 1892 followed a younger brother Lionel to South Africa to help him establish a fruit farm. There Herbert met Cecil Rhodes, who gave him work, and there he made a name for himself as an architect before returning to live at Owletts with his wife and cousin Florence Edmeades.

Herbert added a library for himself and opened up the front hall to create a living room with more fine plasterwork. He commissioned Arts and Crafts workmen and filled the house with artifacts brought home from South Africa. Close to his heart was the preservation of rural England, including Owletts and its cherry orchards. He gave the house and 25 acres to the National Trust in 1939. After his and my grandmother's death, my father took on the tenancy. I took it over in 1984.

It was here that Herbert and his siblings were raised during the prosperous years for yeoman farmers. As the children expanded into the upper floor in the 1870s, they would have watched their father add a north wing, not as well proportioned or generous as the original, to accommodate the servants. Their mother, Frances Georgina, ran the household with a staff of nine[2]. With a Victorian passion for ferns she created a fernery, complete with a boiler stoked daily, hot pipes and hessian to give humidity when splashed with water. Owletts gave the boys space to roam and to indulge their love of sport, both ball games and shooting.

This was the time when families began to record their lives with photography. Children learnt to draw, paint and write diaries, and of course letters were exchanged by the efficient royal mail. Such were the records left by this generation for me to unravel.

Twelve children were born to Thomas Henry and Frances, two girls dying in their infancy:

1854, Henry Edmeades, known as Harry, a career soldier,
1857, Edward Lowther, known as Ned, a Rochester solicitor,
1860, Francis James, known as Frank, an apprentice farmer,
1862, Herbert, then known as Bert, the architect,
1864, Alfred William[3], known as Alf, whose trunk it is,
1866, Beatrice, known as Bee, animal lover, never married. She joined Lionel in Sussex,
1867, Percy Thomas, schoolmaster then solicitor with Ned, and a keen golfer,
1870, Lionel, fruit farmer in the Cape and later in Sussex,
1872, Charles Maurice, civil servant in India, who retired to Meopham,
1876, Arthur George, a surveyor in Kenya.

Herbert and Alfred, c. 1874

My first exploration from the family archive was into the letters sent from Iowa by the third brother, Frank. He died of typhoid in 1881, aged 21, only seven weeks after leaving England on the *S S Celtic.* I flew to Iowa in 2002 and was taken to see the barn where he worked and to the city cemetery to see his gravestone, one of the earliest there.

Having explored the brief life of the third sibling, what about the tin trunk? There was no doubt about who was the owner:

Capt A. W. Baker D. L. I.

The contents looked inviting. The cricket cap and cigar box needed little exploration. Then there was a "hussife" with buttons, pins, needles and thread perhaps made by his mother, which every soldier carried. Quickly I thumbed through lists of cricket scores and of game shot, diaries, notebooks and some delightful sketch books. There were a dozen notebooks and diaries, bank books, game shooting records and "Instructions of Officers in Practical Tactics" from the Indian Army and even a leather writing satchel. His mother Frances Georgina had also kept many of his letters: would all this be enough to tell his story?

I discovered the brothers went to a Dame's School in Rochester and among other skills Alfred developed an ability to draw.

"I wish she would move" A W Baker July 1875

The tin trunk revealed its earliest evidence - an ink drawing, made when Alfred was only 11 with the title "*I wish she would move*", created in July 1875. He captured the detail of the boat's rigging, and I love the humour of the warmly dressed observer unwittingly guarding the clothes of the lone swimmer.

Herbert and Alfred vied with each other at sports and athletics, "like twins," their Mother said. There was plenty of Cricket because their father, Thomas Henry, ran the village team with a game every Saturday and evening practice once a week throughout the summer and he wrote about it (Ref 1). The boys had ample opportunity to play for the village and for Tonbridge School, where Alfred followed Herbert into Judde House in January 1876. Alfred was in the school's Rugby football XV from the age of 15 and at 17 was in the cricket XI under Herbert as captain. He also kept a meticulous list of his score in every cricket game and his averages for each year.

More records in the trunk tell me that at Tonbridge in 1879 he won the under-15 high jump with a leap of 4ft 6½ and the school competition with another of 5ft 6½ in 1882. He was Captain of Rugby football and took second place in eight athletic events in 1882.

That was his last school year. Herbert had left and Alfred was prominent on the cricket field, both as a batsman and a useful second fast bowler. That last cricket season at Tonbridge saw him score 527 runs at an average of 31 and he took 22 wickets at 8.4 runs per wicket. When Herbert returned to the school with a visiting team Alfred had the thrill of having him caught at cover point, one of four wickets he took in the innings.[4] The contents of the trunk were coming into their own.

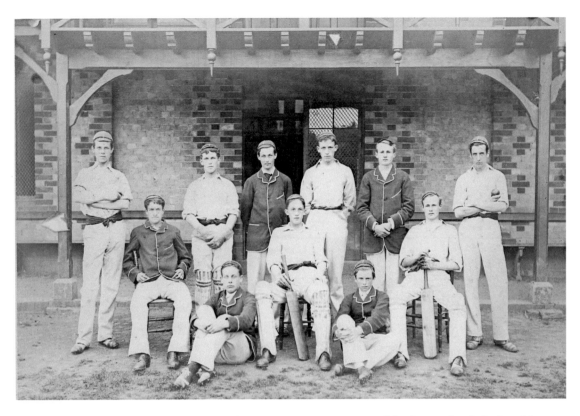

Tonbridge Cricket, 1881. Herbert, Captain in centre, Alfred over his left shoulder.

Prowess on the sports field taught young men to lead. Their academic record was of lesser account: they were capable and strong. Being younger sons, there was neither a farm to inherit nor a parental occupation to follow. Herbert had chosen architecture "because he could draw". Alfred could too, but the physical activity of soldiery was his choice. He was a cadet at the Sandhurst Royal Military Academy for 12 months from February 1883, passing out with good marks in military law, administration, tactics, topography and reconnaissance, fortification, drill, gymnastics and riding. The fee his father paid was £125 and not until he reached the rank of Captain ten years later did Alfred's salary reach that figure[5].

Sandhurst gave him the qualification, but what a young officer needed was a commission into a regiment. Did his Father buy it? The earlier practice of buying a commission had been formally abolished in the 1860s under the Cardwell reforms, but other writers suggest that it had not died out. I could find no suggestion of any payment. Was Alfred of sufficient merit to be offered a commission? Whatever the reasoning, he chose not a Kentish but a newly forming regiment, the Durham Light Infantry. This regiment's 1st Battalion was the former 68th of the British line, established in Durham. The 2nd Battalion, which Alfred joined, had been recently formed from the 106th Foot, originally part of the East India Company's army.

The British Army in 1884 had many commitments; to keep the peace at home, in Africa, in India and it had to be in readiness in all those places. The two battalions of a regiment each had 500 officers and men when at full strength, one "at home" and the other abroad. While "at home" a battalion recruited, trained and prepared itself and after two or three years it would be posted to allow the other battalion home. Alfred as soon as he was commissioned found himself aboard ship to Gibraltar to join his battalion. With a bank account established with Holts' in London[6] to receive his pay, he sailed on the *S. S. Malabar* on 2nd April 1884. He was 20, an officer only 8 weeks.

5

The Rock of Gibraltar, 1885

From Alfred's sketchbook

Alfred's first year of active service was a quiet time for the British garrison and he would have been learning the ropes as a junior officer. Garrison life can quite quickly become humdrum, but his sketches show that he explored the Rock, the Moorish Castle and took time to be precise with pencil and watercolour. I will spare you the bullfight, but among the 15 or so drawings from this time are everyday scenes, perspectives of the buildings and people in the dramatic landscape. Through his eyes we can enjoy Gibraltar a century ago.

And there was cricket. He played 25 games in the summer of 1884 in Gibraltar, against other regiments and civilian teams. Clearly his cricket improved: he scored 850 runs at an average of 33 and took 67 wickets. Here is a sample of his meticulous records. Indeed his enthusiasm caused the DLI to start a regimental cricket book, which Alfred himself kept up for its first few years.

1884.

Date	Match	Runs	Wkts	Place
May 23	Infantry Brigade v Rest	54*	-	Gibraltar
May 30	North v South	{ 1 / 7		"
June 6	Public Schools v Rest	7		"
June 10	Capt. Hughes xi v Civilians	20		"
June 20	Single v Married	53*		"
June 27	Officers v N.C.O's & men	59		"
July 1	2d Durham L.I. v Civilians	{ 38 / 17	6 for 10	"
July 12	2d B: Durham L.I. v 1st Berkshire Reg!	4		"
July 15	2d B: Durham L.I. v R. Dublin Fus:	103	3 for 18	"

Part of Alfred's own cricket record (Diary 3) for 1884

From Alfred's portfolio, undated

In this picture cattle are being driven ashore; the scene could be anywhere until one notices, at the extreme right, the sentry. Is this the view looking north from Gibraltar, with a single guard on duty at the border? If so, how different today; this is the site of the airport. The floating ballerina suggests other distractions from garrison life.

On February 2nd 1885, he sailed on the *S S India* to Genoa. His sketch books show that he spent three weeks in Nice, and two each in Mentone and Bordighera in nearby Italy, where he sketched this frisky horse. Whether he was there to recover from illness or as part of some military exercise is not clear. After a week in Milan he travelled by train via Paris to Owletts and was at home from April to August.

But while Alfred was in England, his battalion was quite suddenly called to Egypt.

From Alfred's portfolio, 1885

Towards The Sudan, 1885

Egypt had been important to Britain for many years because it provided a shorter overland route to India than around The Cape. When Napoleon had threatened this in 1798 Britain was quick to respond, defeating the French at both Alexandria and the Battle of the Nile. By the late 1800s a new threat appeared from the south. Exploited for many years by the Ottoman Empire and by Egypt as a source of taxes, slaves and ivory, the Sudanese resolved to unite and rebel. The catalyst was Muhammad Ahmad, the obscure son of a carpenter, who in 1881 proclaimed himself the Mahdi or Guided One of the Prophet.

He chose an opportune time because Egypt was in chaos as well as in debt. In November 1869, the Suez Canal, built by the Frenchman de Lessops was opened, but left Egypt in debt to France. Britain's Prime Minister, Disraeli, was quick thinking and borrowed money to buy Egypt's share of the canal in 1875. Thus Britain gained an equal control with France and that removed any risk of the French closing the canal for military advantage.

Meanwhile General Gordon, Governor-General of The Sudan, had mapped the Upper Nile in the 1870s, established trade posts and suppressed the slave trade. By 1880 he advised London that Egypt's policy of milking The Sudan could not last. Gladstone, now the prime minister, saw no benefit in imperialist expansion and announced that Britain would not uphold any claim to The Sudan. But Britain would certainly defend Egypt; it would train Egypt's troops and add its own if required to fight the Mahdi.

General Gordon was left in a terrible predicament. All he could do was to assemble his staff and families, British and Egyptian, and prepare to leave Khartoum. He had no troops. He made placatory offers to the Mahdi who chose to ignore, humiliate and eventually starve Gordon out. The disaster of Khartoum was all too obvious long before it happened. After prevaricating, Gladstone sent a relief force up the Nile. It battled the Sudanese with success on more than one occasion, but reached Khartoum too late. Gordon had been killed on his doorstep and a few of his number staggered back to Egypt to tell the tale.

That was in January 1885. In March, Alfred's battalion was summoned from Gibraltar to Egypt, but Alfred himself was by then on his way home. A quiet summer followed for him, with cricket of course, until he was called for training in Newcastle and at a camp at Whitley Bay. Not until October 3rd did he set sail aboard the *S S Deccan* via Ireland for Alexandria, to join his battalion. This is where Alfred's letters start, sent to his Mother or Father or sometimes to a brother or sister and many were kept. The letters often include drawings, and they add to the treasures of the trunk; they let him tell his own story.

He joked from Queenstown (Cork) in Ireland: *my exterior arrived here safely after a beastly passage. As luck will have it I am on duty today and can't get away, else I might have gone to Cork. I am thinking of deserting here, it is so infernally rough.* From Malta: *I've survived the perils of the deep so far. We had a very bad time of it after passing Gib. I have not suffered from seasickness though since the day we left Ireland, but it is very unpleasant all the same tumbling about. We are pretty comfortable on this ship as it is still a P & O and has not been altered much, very crowded though with 1,000 men on board.*[7]

After a week near the mouth of the Nile at Ramleh, he went to a field camp near Cairo called Abbassiyeh. What was the next step to be? His letters echo the Army's grapevine: India?

Called up river? Stay a year? He soon learnt the Army's trick of making the best of the uncertain life. As well as musketry training he was delighted to find some keen cricketers among the 9 or 10 regiments camped nearby: *the cricket season is just commencing and I just got here in time for a match. I played for Cairo against Abbasiyeh and we made 300 for 9 wickets. There are a lot of keen cricketers among the nine or ten regiments... a very decent ground, but an asphalt pitch covered with matting. I did not like it a bit, but get used to it, made 22 yesterday.*[8]

Alfred must have heard plenty of stories of what the Sudanese fighting Dervishes were like. The Dervish had earned a wholesome respect as he had driven both British and Egyptian out of The Sudan apart from Suakin on the Red Sea coast (Ref 2). Kitchener later made it clear; "You are facing the most savage army in the world. The Arab warrior is like Sudan's wild buffalo: if he sees you he will kill you unless you kill him first" (Ref 3). Kipling later summed up the Tommy's attitude in "Fuzzy Wuzzy:

> "We've fought with many men across the seas,
> An' some was brave an' some was not
> The Paythan an' the Zulu an' Burmese,
> But the Fuzzy was the finest of the lot."[9]

To give the military details, Alfred was part of the 1st Brigade of the Frontier Field Force under General Butler. It consisted of English: 52 officers, 1,757 men, 20 horses and 163 camels, plus Egyptian: 12 officers, 255 men, 5 horses and 186 camels.[10] The Force had orders not to reconquer the Sudanese but to keep them out of Egypt. The Mahdi had died and the leadership passed to the Khalifa Abdullahi, who hoped to take the whole of Egypt in retaliation for the years of oppression. But not even Gladstone could risk losing control of the vital route to India.

General Stephenson, who was senior to Butler, had written on December 4th: "Proposed action: withdraw to Wady Halfa after successful encounter with enemy when this can be effected without loss of credit."[11] The message intended for the Sudanese, despite their success at Khartoum and their recent harassing of outposts, was that the British could beat them and would resist any attempt they might make on Egypt.

Alfred wrote home on November 2nd: *we have been ordered up the Nile, probably to Aswan, 500 miles up river. It will take a month to get there. I have been for a donkey ride or two: grand donkeys they have which take the place of cabs.* Two weeks later from Cairo: *Just off up Nile at short notice, awful bustle... A long journey escorting a skein of camels and have not had a square meal all the time, everything packed. The authorities say there is sure to be a row of some sort, small or big they don't know, with 30,000 black chaps knocking about. Wonderful things they fit us up in: putties, spine protectors, goggles, veils. A Tommy was overheard to say they'd only got to be set alight to look like a lot of ... Christmas trees.* [12]

Leaving the citadel at Cairo on November 8th, they travelled by train overnight - *dirty journey, men in open trucks* - to reach Assiout on the Nile. Embarking there, the group of about 750 men was *getting on up the river about 30 miles a day, going from daybreak to dusk, two steamers each towing two barges. Very interesting trip for an antiquarian always coming across some old places. We have been all day here (Luxor) today coaling so that we have been*

9

on shore. I made a couple of donkey rides to Karnak and Thebes: all much the same ruined temples carved all over with those peculiar figures. Wonderful buildings in their way.[13]

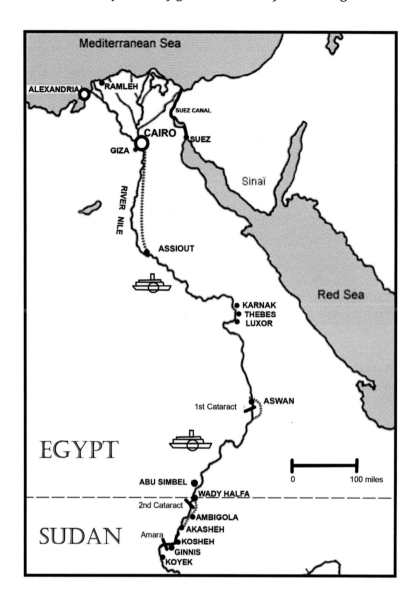

Alfred's journey up The Nile, 1885-86

On November 20th they reached Aswan and early on the 21st marched to a camp, *a place called Tagoog Heights, a bare hill 4 miles from the town. We dwell in mud huts without doors or windows, no roof except palm leaves: very comfortable.* Next day he was back with his men at the riverside to load more baggage on to trains for the short railway loop around the first cataract. On the 23rd *had to go with half the battalion to pull a steamer through the cataract. Hard pulling till 3 pm, got her through with 600 men at work. Corporal drowned in river.*[14]

His open reactions written to his Mother are refreshing. *It is not the climate that knocks people up but hard work on bad food. Rations are bully beef and biscuit: the beef aint' bad but it gets monotonous. Ripping good pay and live cheap: 2 suits of khakee and 2 flannel shirts. Khakee is good stuff, looks smart when it's old with puttees that we always wear.*[15] Evidently this was an early form of khaki as it soon washed almost white.

Alfred's drawing of the camp above Assouan (Aswan)

By December 6th Alfred and the DLI were back on barges above Aswan, *awful cold at night with rats running over you* travelling up to the second cataract at Wady Halfa. From there, on the 10th another railway took them 45 miles to Ambigola. They were to build a fort there, *an awful place, nothing green within sight. The only excitement is the train coming in 3 times a day or an occasional scare that the Arabs are at us. No use holding this beastly place. General Stephenson is coming up today.* Stephenson, then 63, was popular with the troops: he had the courtesy of an earlier age and was liked for his decided opinions and resolve. By Christmas Eve, Alfred was at Akasheh, the end of the railway, *beastly place, sandstorm been raging, eyes and mouth full of dust. We sleep on the sand behind the trenches, had to dig myself out this morning. We are going to have a big battle at Kosheh in a week or less, the niggers are all entrenched there.*[16]

The story picks up in his diary for December 25th 1885: *Slept in exposed sandy place, bad sandstorm all night, smothered with gritty sand. 4 am (an hour before daylight), troops standing to arms. Awfully cold as it had been all night with only 2 blankets. Stood till reveille at day break, 5.50 am breakfast of cold bacon, tea, ration biscuit.*

6.30 embarked in boats. Got a rotten crew, none ever been in a boat before and got carried downstream very nearly over cataract with Colonel and staff shouting at me. N.B. I knew as much about a boat as rest of crew. However got away and my boat passed about 18 others and came in 3rd having started last. Disembarked, loaded camels and started to march to Firket about 13 miles [Firket was 5 miles below Kosheh, see the map on page 14]. *Very bad marching, loose sand. Halted for half an hour at 1 pm for men to get water and have dinner. Had nothing with me, so got no lunch. Reached Firket at dusk about 6.30 pm very tired. Was asked to dinner with Mounted Infantry; refused by Col Lee however who went himself. Was put out on night piquet with my company. Tried to get a dinner for myself worthy of Christmas (had splendid appetite), the Company Sergeant's haversack and canteen of tea made an excellent meal. Supposed to go round my sentries every hour of night. Firket about 6 or 7 miles from enemy's position.*[17]

The Battle of Ginnis, December 1885

The battle was fought on the east bank of the Nile, about 90 miles upstream of Wady Halfa and over 600 miles from the Mediterranean, at the village of Ginnis. It was the northernmost stronghold of the Sudanese who had been harrying the British and Egyptians at Firket. Lord Grenfell (Ref 5), in command of the division which included Butler's brigade, told the story:

"Before dawn on the 30th (December), the Force moved out into the desert under a waning moon, the Great Bear and Southern Cross both conspicuous, and silently took up position. No sound but the barking of dogs was heard from the village below and the Arabs seemed wholly unaware of the coming attack. The General and staff took up their positions on rising ground opposite the village to watch the whole panorama. As the sun rose (behind them but in the Arabs' eyes) the scene unfolded: the endless Libyan desert, the Nile at Kosheh and its sharp bend to the north, rocky islands studding the Amara cataract, fringed with palms.

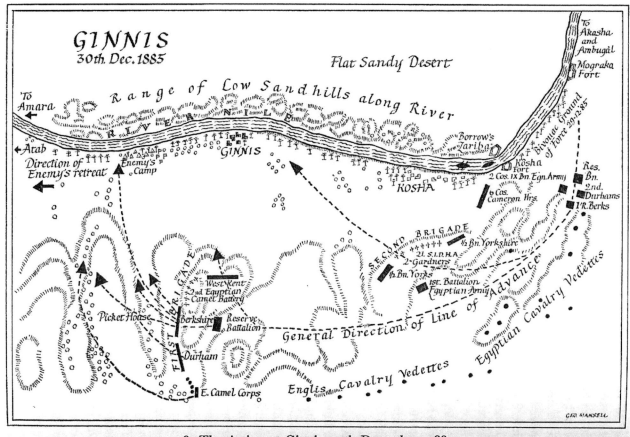

18. The Action at Ginnis, 30th December, 1885

From Ref 6, page 272.

"Butler's brigade had to pass obliquely along the flank of the Arabs' in order to occupy a razor-backed ridge before the Arabs could reach it, making a detour to avoid alarming the Dervish outposts. The Brigade succeeded in gaining the position just in time. The Arabs who had been caught napping, found their camp and Kosheh commanded on all sides. A battery opened fire. The Brigade atop its ridge repulsed an attack. Scots and local troops who had been the garrison in Kosheh and under frequent harassment were straining to go and on the order raced for the village and routed them. By 10 am the battle was won."

Alfred wrote and sketched his own account of the battle three days later when he was further upstream at Koyek. *We halted the night before about 2 miles from the Arabs' position. Up soon after 2 am and did a moonlight march round Kosheh over low rocky hills and about daybreak, 6 am, got near them. I was in command of the leading company and had to skirmish over a range of low hills but we did not find them the other side of it. As soon as we got up the next ridge they opened fire and we extended the line, the Berks on the right, Durham in the centre and the W. Kent on the left, Egyptian camel corps on the extreme left and Egyptian guns on the right. The fire lasted for 4 or 5 hours before we drove them back, advanced after them and took their village of Ginnis. They are plucky chaps and came right at us although we kept up a continuous fire. They don't seem to be much of shots though, as they only hit two officers who were standing up exposed all the time. They had six foot of me to aim at but never hit it. I don't think they had many riflemen among them and the fire was too hot to let their spearmen and swordsmen get near us. We followed them up three days' march, but they seem to have bolted altogether. They may attack us on the way back though.*

Alfred's sketch of the battle of Ginnis

This is a very healthy life, lots of exercise, little to eat and open air all day and night. Nothing but Nile water to drink. The river is a blessing as sleeping in the sand with all your clothes on is apt to make you rather beastly dirty, but I generally manage to get a dip in the river. I have not heard from England. I hope you get my letters as I can never put a stamp on.[18]

Alfred's account and the official report differ a little on the timing, the latter stating tersely:

"Attacked enemy at 6 am, occupied Giniss 9.15 am. Enemy now in full retreat. Enemy taken by surprise, all our troops in position before aware our presence. Butler had the brunt of the fight."[19] It recorded that one British officer was killed, 21 men wounded, 6 Egyptian troops killed, 13 wounded and that the enemy's losses were heavy (later estimated at 500 dead and 300 wounded of a force of 6,000).

Alfred agreed: *the reason we licked them so easily was that we got to their proper position before they did (though only by about 5 minutes).*[20] The three days' march over the New Year following the Dervishes up river took Alfred past Abri where the Nile turns abruptly and on to Koyek. They held that from January 2nd to the 6th and then the tactical withdrawal began. They were back to Kosheh, a little downstream of the battle, by January 9th.

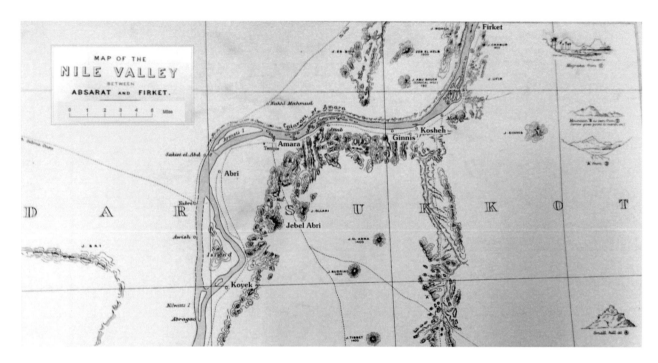

Part of a contemporary map made by the British. PRO MPHH 1 431 29 Abu Sari

A message came up from headquarters in Aswan:
"the Brigadier General (Stephenson) desires to congratulate the Force under his Command upon the fact that yesterday's action was fought in the old English Formation of Line, and that the Brigade inflicted a crushing defeat upon the Enemy, captured his Guns, Camp and Standards, and routed the entire Arab Army from its strong position."[21]

After the Battle, 1886

The excitement over, the soldier's life settled down to manning the outpost of Kosheh. They were employed cutting down palm trees and destroying the village that had been an advance post of the enemy.

By the end of January Alfred and his fellow officers had a mess going, ordering what they wanted to come up river. He praised some enterprising Greeks who appeared with condensed milk, bread, meat and jam, at a price, but welcome. He could be terse too. Writing to his parents: *I wish you would finish those elections in England and decide what to do with this place. It is heartily detested by all troops and is not worth holding. You have formed too high an opinion of Egypt; it is not a country at all but a river and 40 yards each side to grow crops and date palms (there is a tax of 9d a year on each palm tree). If you come to settle out here as you talked about bring a water-can.*[22] He was echoing an Arab saying "when Allah made The Sudan, he laughed".

Alfred's sketch of a sunset, possibly looking upstream to Jebel Abri from Kosheh. January 1886
The village of Ginnis would be on the left of this scene.

By now sickness was rife and *summer would be awful.* Within a week they were building mud huts for the whole regiment, *bricks without straw.* Ever the sportsman, Alfred wrote to his brother Herbert, then in a London architect's office:

I have been trying to discover the ways of the game. Gazelle come in threes and fours down the mullahs to feed in the early morning and evening. Wild geese sit in pairs on the rocks out in the stream all day and feed on the banks at night. Sandgrouse come down to the river from the desert every morning at 9 o'clock, have a drink and go back regular as clockwork: like partridges, bigger with shaped wings for flying long distances. The only other things are rock doves and a sort of silly plover.

We have started a hunt here; one meet so far. The pariah dog is the fox and the game is to ride him down. It gives a first-rate gallop. Mules are first rate and would think nothing of going down the cliffs of Dover. We have also a race meeting: I shall go for the mule steeplechase.[23]

By mid February, *we are building ourselves mud huts instead of knocking down Arab ones. A wonderful variety of skills I'm picking up; cutting trees and building, not to mention a little in the nautical line. We have cut down all the palm trees and levelled the houses for about 1½ miles in front of our position and stuck up two small forts.*[24] *I have found a dodge for getting sandgrouse, by going out to a sandbank at 8.30 in the morning. They come down as regularly as possible about 9 o'clock for a drink. I got 4 yesterday; they make a variety in the diet.*[25] In one of the notebooks he listed the game he had shot in those three months at Kosheh: 11 sandgrouse, 26 partridge, 4 (Blacksmith?) plover, a goose, 2 snipe, 5 pigeons and even a pelican[26]. Later, *the race meeting was a success. I rode in a mule race and after a desperate finish saved being last by a head.*

1886 sketch by Alfred of the forts they built at Firket

As before there were rumours of staying, of going further up river, or of being posted on to India. Anything would be *better than knocking about here. I expect we shall grumble just the same. I believe if we were quartered in paradise everyone would grumble.* He calculated that 11 of their 17 officers had been on the sick list, others including himself bad at times. Nothing wrong with his humour though: *fashionable here now: any amount of ex MPs and other globetrotters visiting the battlefield. They generally go back quicker than they come though; get sick.* Also: *The doctor has just gone sick so we shall have a chance.*[27]

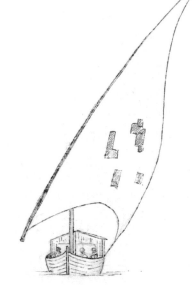

In March Alfred and another officer were called downstream to Wady Halfa to take an exam. Leaving Kosheh by camel to take the boat, they lost their way, missed the boat, took fresh camels and rode on, 30 to 40 miles to the railway at Akasheh. Next day 87 miles in a jolting train. A month later, back at Kosheh he heard they were to withdraw downstream, following the policy decisions of December. Everyone was thankful as disease was taking an undue toll. The seasonal drop in the level of the Nile was expected to restrict boat movement, hence the sudden haste. Alfred reported the Army chatter: *the niggers are trying to turn it off up above.*[28] He had passed his exam, was proud not to be on the sick list and only too thankful to be leaving.

A Nile nuggar, able to carry 20 tons of freight[29]

A week later he was still at Kosheh, packing up all the stores and getting them by camel to a navigable stretch of the river. The huts recently built were all to be blown up, but *they can't make us plant the palm trees again.* Captured caravans were sold back to the Sudanese. They moved down river, blowing up or burning anything of use and not portable: huts, boats and the railway.

No amusement but I have the skin of a Green Bee-eater for you. Two days later: *cannot send the bird so enclose flower of cotton-bush. Yours perspiringly.. A W Baker.*[30]

Alfred's regiment was the last to leave; he had to load camels all morning on April 29th and then march to the river. It was a gloomy business burying two men a day and sending many home sick, as the temperature reached 120F.

Abu Simbel: Alfred's comment: *one of their fingers is about as big as I am.*

They were soon back in the stern-wheelers towing barges down to Aswan. *I am boss-man of one and will contrive to get wrecked at convenient spots.* Sure enough: *ran aground 50 times and one steamer wrecked.* The gloom got to him as he signed off expecting the Dervishes to take advantage of their retreat: *you will hear soon of the massacre of the garrison at W Halfa. I am the remains of (skin and bone) A W Baker.*[31]

Aswan seems to have been better provisioned: *...beginning to get fat again. I can understand the good will in the saying "May your shadow never grow less". I wish I had Bert here: it would puzzle him to find something to do.* All Alfred found was a walk and a tub in the evenings. He dared not hope for leave as the number of officers, supposed to be at least a dozen out of the full-strength 25, was down to eight or so due to sickness. One letter ends: *enclosed a young scorpion; don't touch his tail. I caught this joker at breakfast. Off to funeral...*

Bought a gee the other day for £10, necessary as they put me on courts martial 5 miles from here. Made rather a good bargain too, shall get more for him if we are relieved. We take turns with the 19th to bury men from hospital – four last night – heavy work.[32]

Very soon he was able to sell his horse at a profit, because he was offered an escape from Egypt: *I am going to get out of this place for a time. Have to take a party of men, not sick but those most likely to die if left here. I am lucky enough to have got the job of taking them to Ramleh.*[33] Once there: *You can't imagine the change after being up river; trees and ladies with white faces and much cooler.*[34] And cricket! *Played one game on a pavement in the midst of sand and received one ball which proved sufficient as I hit it too high,*[35] a modest account as his notebook also recorded that he took 3 wickets for 16 runs.

Alfred was now on his way out of Egypt. He was in charge of 130 men from various regiments of the Nile force. They sailed from Alexandria to Limasol in Cyprus on June 18th 1886. They were well out of it as up river: *the Dorsets suffered worst, 1,000 went up and 400 will come down. All who died are under 24, but it seems to be the old men who fill themselves with beer every night who die of heat apoplexy.*[36]

As soon as they reached Cyprus they travelled up to Troödos near Mount Olympus: *rather a different place than Aswan ... on mules and donkeys, a hundred men at a time. All travelling by night starting when the moon rose. Took us four nights. We are bang on top of the mountain, 6000 feet I believe. We form part of the convalescent depot for Egypt men, 700 in all. Swarms with poisonous snakes they say; all the natives wear knee high boots, men and women alike. Couldn't make out the object of the boots till I was told, not much chance of a flood up here. By the way where is this island? I wish you would send me a map of Europe.*

The water is the finest thing, like soda water, a change from hot green muddy Nile water. Greek was a new challenge: *I had just mastered Arabic. They don't understand me, tried to bargain for a* ἵππος *the other day without seeing the animal. Knocked him down to 2 bob when the chap brought me a teapot. Evidently ancient and modern Greek are different.* But there was cricket an hour's walk up the mountain where he captained The Convalescents v. the Berkshires winning by 11 runs[37].

We cannot let Alfred depart from The Sudan without a word of what happened next in the region. The Khalifa and his Dervishes held sway in The Sudan until 1896, a full ten years after the battle of Ginnis. Though their threat to Egypt was undiminished, they turned more attention eastward to Abyssinia. Kitchener, who had gained fame for his part in the failed attempt to rescue Gordon, had been in charge of the British forces on the Red sea coast of The Sudan at the time of Ginnis. He was appointed Sirdar (Commander in Chief) of the Egyptian Army in 1892. He rigorously reorganised it, with a view to retaking The Sudan. Britain may well have left The Sudan alone had not France moved towards the sources of the Nile and the Italians, attacked by Dervishes in Abyssinia, asked for military help. In 1896 Kitchener won two battles due to superior weaponry and his efficient organisation which included the laying of 500 miles of railway above Wady Halfa to supply the troops. The decisive battle was at Omdurman. Kitchener then reoccupied Khartoum in September 1896 avenging General Gordon (Ref 7) and he came to an agreement with the French general and both could withdraw.

If there were more letters from Alfred in Cyprus after July 1886 they have not survived. From his own list of dates and places, he left the island in October with his contingent now in better health, returned to Alexandria for a week before shipping back to England. 400 men of the DLI including Alfred were transferred at this point to the 1st Battalion, which had come

from India to form part of the garrison at Colchester, while the 2nd Battalion sailed on from Suez to India to be stationed at Poona (Ref 8). Alfred reached England on November 16th, 1886.

Those at the battle of Ginnis were presented with two medals: the Egyptian medal and the Khedive Star. The Khedive was the traditional ruler of Egypt, a title sometimes assumed by the British. The medal ceremony for the DLI took place on December 17th 1886, in Cairo. Alfred was not present but certainly received his medals and wore them (see photo on page 25). Alas, they have not been kept with his papers in the trunk.

The Khedive Star 1886 with thanks to
Spinks British Battles and Medals

England, 1887 to 1889

Though there are no letters from this period, the thread of Alfred's life in England can be kept alive by his sporting records. In 1887 he played cricket 18 times with the DLI, scoring 500 runs, including one century, with an average of 31.3 and he took 30 wickets. Perhaps it was for this success that he received a small gun-metal shield, found in the trunk with his sketchbooks. I imagine it would have been riveted to a cup or cup stand and is inscribed:

Presented to A W Baker Esq DLI
by Mr Briggs for best
batting averages, 1887

Alfred in working uniform with medal ribbons

When he was not playing for the regiment it was for the Colchester garrison (where he made another century) or the Colchester and East Essex team. Back at Tonbridge in July he played for the old boys and at home for Cobham against the Royal Engineers, scoring 52.

The following year, 1888, saw him back in the barracks in Newcastle and playing now for Northumberland every week in May and June. From mid July to mid September he played three matches a fortnight, travelling all over Tyneside. 1889 seems to have been the climax, when he played 27 times for Northumberland, some on a tour with the team as far afield as Yorkshire, Norwich, Northampton and finally Lord's, where he scored 10 against an MCC team. From May to September there were games for the Regiment or the Garrison up and down Northumberland and Durham.[38] The last entry was a game in December 1889, but that was in Suez. Alfred was back with the 2nd Battalion and on his way to India.

Sport and Sketching: India, 1890 – 93

The British had been many years in India by the time Alfred reached Bombay. India was such a source of wealth with cotton, silk, tea, salt, spices etc being traded between Europe, India and China, that an Army was kept to preserve the routes of trade, both land and sea. By 1889, internal transport was being developed and the map shows how extensive a rail network the British built. The army could respond should the Mutiny of 1857 recur or if troops were needed in Afghanistan where Russia and Britain might clash. Alfred's records of his movements about the country show that he spent many hours on those trains. Troops were deliberately moved allowing each regiment its share of the good postings as well as the difficult. They took the opportunity to arrange shooting competitions and polo.

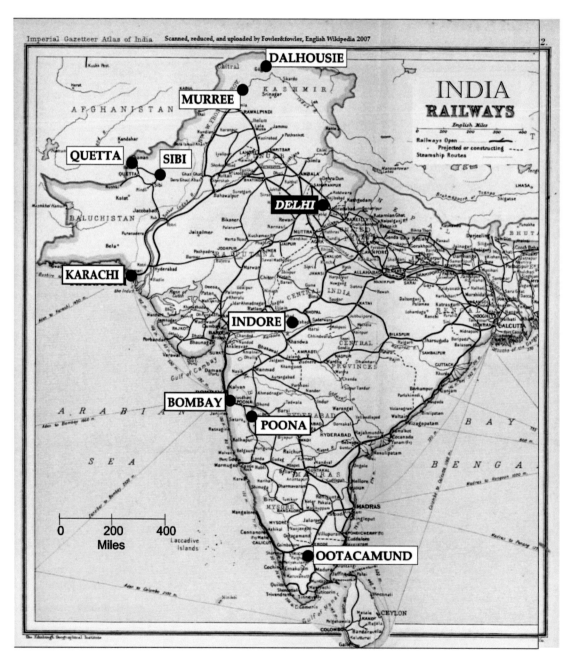

India's Rail Network (1909), showing where Alfred served, 1890 - 93

Twenty years earlier the Indian Army had assimilated that of the old East India Company and applied a rule of at least one European to two Indian soldiers. Alfred didn't write of his military work. The trunk revealed certificates from courses he took to qualify as a mounted infantry officer and as a signalling and musketry instructor[39]. He taught Indians as well as British. Otherwise it was a waiting game and he made the best of it.

Arriving in Poona in January 1890, Alfred was immediately in his element: shooting in January quickly moved to cricket and *I take twice the exercise I used to in England; early evening go up river, getting rather an oarsman, racing form almost...*[40]

Parvati from Alfred's letter 1890 02 16. He claimed that at the spot marked Prince Albert (later the Duke of Clarence) and his wife were pitched off an elephant.

Three weeks later on exercise at Wanowrie, three miles south of Poona he made this delightful sketch from his tent of the Parbutti (now Parvati) temples on their hilltop. But he was expecting to be on the move again: Quetta in March, *unpromising*, he wrote beforehand, *snow there and now raining hard we hear.* Getting there meant 100 miles by rail to Bombay, a sea voyage of three nights to Karachi, then 500 more miles by rail, tedious no doubt. Though his cricket records show us where he was month by month there is no letter surviving until July. He had left Quetta for Kashmir.

He wrote to his sister from "Snow view", Dalhousie in July 1890, with cheery humour: *little to do except peacocking about after uninteresting females on the tennis courts or ball room. Racquet court shut and no cricket, now it rains all day and every day. I do a lot of walking up the cliffs here as I have not got a pony... tried one but found I could carry him not he me.*

I brought my dog, a stray I picked up in Quetta, a fox terrier a little long in the leg and very pretty head, only like all natives his face is black. There were two swallows building in his bedroom: *they wake me every morning at 6 to let them out. They had a great fight this morning with two others who came in. Feathers and swallows were falling on my bed for half an hour when the intruders got the boot.*[41] He sent fern specimens to his mother.

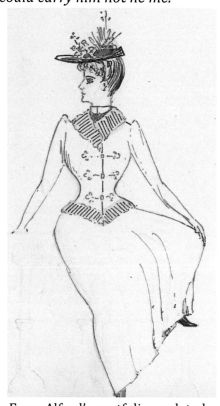

Back in Quetta, 5,000 feet up on the border of Afghanistan and hot and dry in August, there was regular cricket for two months. In October he wrote to his sister Bee to say he had a touch of fever, but he was able to buy a pony: *the first I have found up to my weight and he is strong enough to carry me at polo. At present he is rough just having come in from Kabul. A pony is not much use here except for polo as the country is uninteresting and not safe, though a little shooting.* There were two kinds of partridge, sandgrouse and teal. *India suits me well enough but I shall never prefer it to England.*

From Alfred's portfolio, undated

In November there was a flood, *but today is lovely, out all morning riding. ... I have been trying to be too young; not content with football, I ran in a paperchase yesterday and can't move today from stiffness. Came in 2nd though.* His sense of irony has not left him: *the only spinster in the place is to be married tomorrow, temporary insanity on the part of the future bridegroom. Glad to hear of all the marriages at home; congratulate them from me.*

By January 1891, *my pony has turned out a clipper, won't make a racer as he carries 14 stone but ought to do well for polo.* Alfred was confined by winter inactivity and *one's ideas get cramped, cut off as we are from all the world.*[42] But he could use the time to study with a view to gaining the rank of Captain. *I passed my examinations with a certain amount of credit, but I see no chance of promotion for some time.*[43]   Indeed none came for two years.

The 2nd was the less well known of the two DLI battalions when it reached India, but it won a high reputation there in the 1890s, largely on the polo field. If a unit did well at polo, it could be trusted in battle. The leading light was a Guernseyman, H de B de Lisle, who had distinguished himself in The Sudan.[44] Alfred and de Lisle were the same age and would have known each other at the battle of Ginnis and later at Colchester in 1886-7. De Lisle had an ability to choose and train ponies and he developed the Battalion's teamwork. An early success was in 1891 at an Open Tournament at Quetta. Alfred was there then and must surely have taken part. Though the trunk has records of the game he bagged and his cricket, I could find no detailed records of polo.

Letters from home were crucial and he was cheered by one from his aunt, his mother's sister Sarah Miller, who lived close to Owletts. There is a delightful rapport: *thank you for a long letter, full of infinite jest. It was not you who wrote nonsense of me basking in the sun fanned to sleep by dusky maidens. The facts are as follows. I have spent the day crouched over a fire, my head tied up in a bag owing to toothache and with devil a dusky maiden about the premises. Coal is 96 shillings a ton and bad, wood nearly used up and priceless. Only news a spinster who came to stay has been snapped up by the best looking subaltern. Ladies wait only a week here with 3,000 white bachelors and one spinster. Couldn't you come and bring some?* [45]

In March 1891 he was back in Poona for three months, then Quetta again from June to August. It was summer, with cricket at least once a week. He seems to have been more valuable with ball than bat, averaging 3 wickets an innings. In early September he travelled again this time further north to the Kashmir border for two months. He gave no hint of any military reason but recorded yet more cricket. He was also after pheasant and chukar partridge, but found more success in official shooting: writing to his mother: *we won the Chief's simultaneous match prize this week, competed for all over India, 150 entries. The score made a record for rifle shooting I believe. He was very fit, too much so and waxing very fat.* [46]

Alfred's Christmas 1891 letter to his aunt Sarah was written from Sibi, then little more than a railway station in the desert at the bottom of the pass below Quetta: *I am here with a depot of convalescents from Quetta, men who could not stand the cold up there. I came down of my own choice, the idea being perfect peace and fair shooting. I am getting both: snipe, black partridge and 3 sorts of grouse.* [47]

Sibi, 1891

23

In the spring of 1892, Alfred returned from Sibi by train to Karachi, ship to Bombay and up to Mhow, near Indore in what is now Madhya Pradesh.[48] He was there a full year.

From Mhow it was not far back to Poona in June for a musketry class: *eight days to put them through the course.* There was an exercise for a visiting duke, manoeuvring in the jungle for two days and a night. *I paraded 6.30 am Tuesday to 6.30 pm Wednesday being on the tramp more or less the whole time. I had to do the picquet and repel night attacks. On Thursday began shooting 6.30 to 11 am then a cricket match till dark, bowling or batting nearly the whole time. I think that put me right as I feel extremely fit again now. Soldiering out here is no joke, not half what it is made out. It is about as hot as they make it now I think, but summer does not begin until tomorrow.*

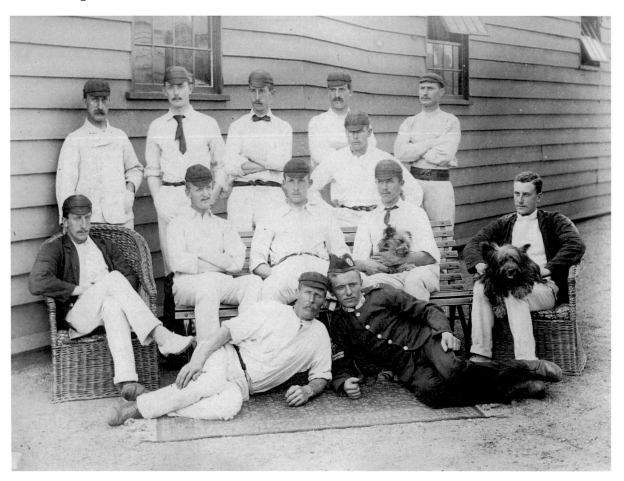

In the DLI's records I was pleased to find this fine photograph of Alfred, centre stage of a cricket team and therefore its captain.[49] This might be the match he recorded at Mhow on 13th September 1892 when A W Baker's XI played against Capt Wilken's XI. Perhaps the humourless faces remind us how they had to pose stock-still for the camera. His cricket records tell us that his team played against local teams as well as other units of the British Army. Two games for example were recorded in Indore in February 1893 as "Indore v Mahomedans" and "Det v Mahomedans".

One thing will have pleased him; there is a note in the trunk signed by De Lisle: "All 20 native signallers exercised by you in Army Signalling, 21 March 1893, have been declared efficient." And life was not so bad: *just been watching my valet cooking. He only uses two stones and a tin pot and a little wood and turns me out a capital dinner of five or six courses; can't think how he does it. Soup just coming in so goodbye for the present.* [50]

Sibi fort, 1892

In April 1893 Alfred at last received promotion to Captain, bringing more pay and more status. It was time to leave India but he had seven weeks before sailing. Since I first opened the tin trunk 110 years after this promotion, I have been puzzled about who made it. It has no maker's mark, but is carefully made with brass chains, a lock and leather padding stuck to the lid to form a seal when closed. Was it hand-made for him? A second clue is the name painted outside: I can see no trace of "Capt" overwriting "Lt", his earlier rank, leading me to conjecture that he bought it in India in the seven weeks between his promotion and his sailing home to England in early June.[51]

He arrived home on June 20th. Two days later he was playing cricket again for Cobham. Thomas Henry would have relished his son's return not only to the family but to the village cricket he had been running for so many years (Ref 1). After a month at home, Alfred was transferred again to the DLI's 1st Battalion, then in Aldershot to practice manoeuvres before embarking for Ireland in September. They arrived at Queenstown, now Cork, on October 2nd 1893 (Ref 8).

Alfred in DLI Captain's
dress uniform

Ireland and England, 1893 - 98

The next gems found in the trunk are a pair of "Pocket Game Registers", both dated 1895-96, issued by the "E. C. Powder Company" of Eyeworth in Hampshire, with instructions on loading, the cost of a gun licence (£3) and the dates of the seasons. Here is a typical page with Alfred's records of his days in the field:

DATE 1894	GROUND SHOT OVER AND PARTY.	Pheasants.	Partridges.	Grouse.	Black Game.	Woodcock.	Snipe.	Wild Fowl.	Hares.	Rabbits.	TOTAL.	REMARKS, HOW DISPOSED OF, &c.
Aug. 13th	3 Brazier Creagh, J. Fitzgerald, J. Cumming J. Smyth self	.	.	6	.	.	.	.	5	.	11	Ballyhoura Mts.
Oct. 23	Adml Nicholson, Genl Edmeades, J. Smacks, T.H.B, H.F.B self	28	2	.	.	.	.	.	20	2	52	Owletts
,, 25	W.S. Masters Capt C.B. H.F.B self	23	5	.	.	.	.	.	4	35	67	Owletts
,, 26	J. Scruton H.F.B self	.	.	.	.	.	.	.	.	83	83	Owletts
,, 27	H.F.B self	4	5	.	.	.	.	.	1	4	14	Owletts
,, 29	Adml Nicholson Genl Edmeades J.F.E self	.	.	.	.	.	.	.	.	31	31	Nurstead
,, 31	W.S. Masters & self	.	4	.	.	1	.	.	.	11	16	Camer

The Gun Club International Cup has been won five out of six times with "E.C." Powder in both barrels, viz.: in 1890, 1891, 1893, 1894 and 1895.

Now a captain, Alfred was in charge of a company, which in practical terms in peace time meant running a training school at a camp at Buttevant, Co Cork: *rather busy getting a big draft ready for India. They start next week. I half wish I was going it's so cold here.*[52] He threw himself into work and the shooting: there was an opportunity two or three times a week in a wild part of Ireland and his colleagues were keen too. After little variety at home (usually pheasants, partridge and rabbits with his brothers and the Edmeades), Ireland offered snipe and duck as well as hare.[53]

The 1894 cricket season gave him lots of scope: a game twice a week and he amassed 1393 runs and took 52 wickets, impressive figures again.[54] He was home for two weeks in June to play for Cobham and the old boys at Tonbridge and again for two months from October to December, but was back in Ireland for Christmas. This time he was posted to Tralee. He liked Tralee: *having a very good time and like the place, hospitable, the ladies of all classes beautiful. The shooting is good and I am getting as much as I can manage.* To remind us of the other side of Irish life, he added: *they condemned a man to be hanged yesterday who came from the village where our shooting is. The keeper was a witness against him and they say is sure to be dead in a month in consequence. It is in the wildest part of the country....*[55]

The seasons of cricket and shooting continued through 1894 to 1897, including a short season for grouse in August 95 in the southern Irish highlands. Despite all the hospitality and no doubt expense, one letter showed some frustration. Written from Dublin one spring he acknowledged a "tip", ie some pocket money his mother sent: *thankfully received. Only don't worry about me if you are hard up.* He found Dublin expensive despite a captain's pay and *I must be out of it... Little chance of getting to Egypt as better men have been passed over.*[56]

Since he was promoted to Captain in 1893, Alfred's pay was 11/3d a day, almost double the 6/6d of a Lieutenant. It's his bank book that reveals this information. But it shows something more: his father Thomas Henry was also contributing a regular £20 or sometimes £35 three times a year in 1884 and 85, nothing in 86 or 87, but it resumed in 1888. There are no records for 1890 or 91 but the contributions were still coming in July 1893.[57] I find these payments interesting because the 1880s and 90s were a long period of economic stress for English farmers. Markets were depressed by improved transport and refrigerated ships that could bring meat and grain from overseas and push prices down. Thomas Henry had started to accumulate debt, borrowing first from the bank and then from his neighbours. Elsewhere Alfred's brother Lionel too was making calls on the home purse: £600 was lent to him by Thomas Henry to buy a share in a South African farm in 1893. There was a payment to Alfred in May 1894. It was not until early 1895 when the other brother Herbert was making enough as an architect in South Africa to send contributions home that the position eased.[58] But matters had become critical by 1896 and the first tranche of Owletts land was sold. Alfred would have known of the straitening circumstances, but he did not acknowledge that until 1898 when more land was sold: *sorry my profession is not a money making one to enable me to help.*[59]

Alfred had asked his eldest brother Harry, retired from the Rifle Regiment, to recommend him to Kitchener's Egyptian Army, which was trained and partly officered by the British and which set off into The Sudan in 1896, but to no avail. The attraction of course was the pay. However he had been appointed captain of cricket of both the regimental and garrison XIs. The cricket he recorded for 1895 was all in Ireland, but after that season his records dry up and I was unable to find others in the DLI records.[60] Did the responsibility of being captain take the energy from his statistical mind?

The last record of his being in Ireland is in October 1895. The absence of cricket records and of letters home leaves us with shooting records only, all in Kent, for 1896 and in both Kent and the north in 1897. More unusual among these are five "landrail" (corncrake) shot in Cumberland in early September 1897 and 38 (red) grouse in Kielder later that month. After four days shooting in Ayrshire in early October, the records are all in Kent apart from 2 days in January 1898 near Newcastle.

Studio photograph by
Guy and Co Ltd of Cork

Nigeria, 1898

The tin trunk next produced a notice that appeared in a Newcastle paper in late 1897:

... the command of a regiment now being raised for service in West Africa, in the Lagos Hinterland, has been offered to and accepted by Major H S Fitzgerald, 1st Batt the Durham Light Infantry. He will be accompanied by Capt. Baker of the same regiment now quartered at Newcastle-upon-Tyne and some 27 officers collected from various battalions of the regular army. The regiment will form part of the expeditionary force under Major Lugard CB, DSO. Their objective is not yet known. It is expected the officers will be absent at least a year.

Nigeria in the 1890s

Southern Nigeria was not declared a British protectorate until 1900, nor was there such a thing as a postage stamp. So why was the military there? Europeans thought they could divide Africa by sphere of influence, but the real chief of the northern three quarters of what would become Nigeria was the Caliph of Sokoto. He ruled an empire stretching 1,000 miles from Ghana east to Lake Chad, with at least 30 emirates and more slaves than North and South America together. Sixty years earlier in 1834 Britain had declared an end to slavery and in 1841 a "model farm" was started on the Niger at Lokoja, to help former slaves to become self-sufficient. It was short-lived because the white men who set it up suffered all too quickly from disease. An exception was George Goldie, who lived to the ripe old age of 80. Goldie traded with the tribes of the rivers Niger and Benue, sufficient for Britain to give his enterprise a charter, the Royal Niger Company, and to declare that its sphere of influence covered the central belt.

By the same agreement France took the western (now Benin and Upper Volta) and Germany the eastern districts (now Cameroun), but the boundaries ran only a certain distance inland. Beyond that, a treaty with a tribe was fair game to the Europeans who got there first. The French spread eastward and the British westward, the overlapping known by Chamberlain as the "chessboard policy" (Ref 9). The European companies pursued trade and if others seemed to push the boundaries they called foul to their government, which would react by sending in the military.

A journalist, who journeyed up the Niger two months before Alfred, commented: "Slavery with its accompanying cruelties is a long way from being ended; indeed slaves form the only currency that is understood. Coins are of no value here, barter is the rule: cloth, cowries etc for small sums, slaves for large."[61] Although the Caliphate was not about to give up its lucrative slaves, it was keen to trade. Enterprising European traders met that need, but had to ask for help on occasion to keep other Europeans at bay. This was where the British and French brought in soldiery, who in turn saw the value of the ex-slaves either to form a local army or to be carriers and workers. The local emirs accused the British of stealing slaves; they could pursue a slave through an Islamic court, but not a colonial one since Britain did not recognise slavery. The emirs found they had to make agreements sooner or later. Into this steamy world came Alfred.

From Alfred's diary, Lokoja, April 1898

An official despatch from the Colonial Secretary Joseph Chamberlain to Britain's Governor of Nigeria, Major Henry McCallum, stated in July 1897:

> ... the representations addressed to the French Government having failed to induce them to withdraw their forces from Boussa and other places, claimed under treaties with native authorities as falling within the British sphere of interest in W Africa, His Majesty's Government have been compelled to consider what steps should be taken to procure the evacuation from those places and to prevent further aggression from the French.

Britain claimed the "land behind Lagos as far as the 9th parallel of north latitude" and that that had been recognised by France in 1889. However there was reason to think that this boundary was not being respected. The French had occupied Benin between 8th and 9th parallels west of the Niger and were looking to the east as well. British posts were needed around Kyama between Nikki and Boussa unless already in French hands. We shall see that Alfred's job also entailed recruiting and training Hausa tribesmen as soldiers and so it is interesting to read Governor McCallum's comment to Chamberlain[62]:

> ...It would never do for the Chiefs and people of the interior to think that we hold out any inducement for Hausa slaves to leave their masters, as that would shake their faith in our integrity. These slaves are so well treated as a rule and have so much time at their disposal that the majority will prefer to remain where they are than exchange for a life of restraint and discipline.

McCallum nevertheless suggested a Hausa battalion as well as a Yoruba (each with six British officers). He even prescribed red forage caps with chin straps for the Hausas in place of the fezzes and tassels for the Yorubas and consulted with others about their fifes and drums. The British were nothing if not thorough in their conception of what an army was.[63]

While the main group of Lugard's West African Frontier Force left Liverpool on February 5th, 1898, Alfred and some others sailed 10 days behind them on the *S. S. Boona* leaving on the 16th. They called at Tenerife on the 24th and reached Forcados at one of the many mouths of the River Niger on March 7th. Transferring at once to the *S S Liberty*, a stern-wheeler, they continued to Burutu, where Alfred hired *one good servant, Edward, wages 5/- a month*, 15 years old and trained by a mission. He spoke English and knew his job. Alfred dined with the agent, *who poor chap died of blackwater fever the next night, as have since all the other white men who were there, (despite) saying he had had it before and knew what to do if he felt it coming on.*[64] They proceeded upstream, reaching Lokoja by March 18th. Alfred at once wrote home: a*t last we have arrived at our goal and a most damnable place it is now we have got here.... You should see us now: ten of the pick of the officers of the British Army are here packed into a mud hut, such as one's native servants live in in India, drinking warm whiskey and water. Temperature in the shade in a draught 98 degrees and a tornado threatening which will probably walk off with the hut.* He was not under any illusions: *the death rate of the (Niger) Company's white employees for the last year is 26 out of 56.*[65]

Got nothing to do here yet, got no men. Had a church parade and being the senior officer in the whole place I had to do parson. He was as usual shooting for the pot: *partridge, guinea fowl and a sort of grouse close to camp. I brought up 200 of these fellows as curriers. They are cannibals... They are capital fellows though and full of fun, but I don't quite like the way they eye me at dinner time.*

By month end, *I have had my head shaved to the skin like a monk and am covered with bites and prickly heat but they don't bother me a bit. There are redeeming features – one does not get enteric or cholera – living as we do here. In India we should all have had them long ago.*

He was drinking beer rather than tea and taking quinine. He was up at 3 am by choice to shoot and during a month at Lokoja his tally was 50 birds: Guinea fowl, partridge or francolin and sand grouse with an occasional pigeon or plover, all no doubt welcome additions to the pot. [66]

Lugard arrived on April 13th. Alfred was to proceed at once by steamer to Jebba, while other groups were to stay at Lokoja or Ibadan, though action was not expected until after the rains. *I am glad we go to Jebba; it is healthier than this, temperatures reaching 106F. I think old age an advantage* (he was 33). He was taking his 5 to 10 grams of quinine a day and *losing weight nicely.*[67]

We eight officers and 12 NCOs are on the way up river to Jebba, 250 miles above Lokoja. We go to start a camp there for the 2nd battalion of the force while the 1st stayed at Lokoja. There was trouble about: *the place we are just passing was slave-raided last night. The refugees are on the opposite bank putting up shelters, their town destroyed by the Bida people, many killed and a lot of slaves taken.*

In his sketch are a marabou stork, cranes, a stilt, geese, a wattled plover and snipe.[68]

On the 18th pausing at spot called Lah in the heat of the day, Alfred, nothing daunted: *picking up a man who knew the bush and two of his friends I started. The bush had partly burnt for some miles by the river and the ground was covered by a foot of black dust. Where not burnt, grass 7 feet high, matted and well nigh impenetrable.*

Here and there one came on small pools of water and stinking ooze covered with water lilies and water birds of all sorts, known and unknown. I shot only duck, geese and teal. There were almost white geese, black duck, grey duck, black and white geese and pygmy geese. I never felt so tired before in my life, my face arms and shirt just as black as my niggers. However I got so keen that I would have missed the ship if it had started on time.

They reached Jebba on April 20th: *ordered to camp on island. Had about the worst time of it I ever remember for the next month, living in small tents on bare rock.*

Heat awful by day, no shade, had to wear hat inside tent. Tornado nearly every night, wet through often.[69] On the 27th he wrote to his mother, *in my new official capacity as Station Staff Officer to the WAFF* (West Africa Frontier Force). *I would rather have my company and get to business.*[70]

In contrast by May 1st his diary displays a more buoyant mood after taking two days to shoot up river with a fellow officer: *went out at daybreak, shot left bank of the Niger.* They camped on an island, but found they had left their food box behind: *I fortunately had a piece of chocolate, a crust of bread and 2 bottles of soda. Divided this, sent canoe back for food and went to bed.* Next day: *bagged a warthog, not trophy but good to feed canoe men. Had a bathe and returned to Jebba by moonlight, pleasant floating*

downstream with whisky and soda and cigar, accompanied by his faithful dog, Lucifer.

I may go off any day. There is no mail service above here to speak of and I am in charge of it, so if you don't get a letter for six months or so, don't be alarmed.

The letter from Alfred of May 7th was written on Owletts' stationary. Apparently his father was both sending out the materials and paying 2½d a letter postage due as Alfred had no way of paying postage.

Though told not to give military information in private letters, Alfred wrote on May 8th:
I probably start at daybreak tomorrow with one subaltern, two Maxim guns and two months' rations in HMS Jackdaw, a river gunboat, 2 days journey to Badgibo. I leave the river for Gongekoko. Last letter for a long time.[71] But a week later he wrote again from Jebba: *still here as the Maxims have not come. We surmise the gunboat stuck in the lower river, 12 days overdue.* That was not the only hazard; a subaltern newly arrived *went to bathe when it was nearly dark. He was seen to dive in by a black boy and not come up again. We found his body in about an hour before the crocodiles. He had hit his head against a rock, stunned himself and was drowned.*[72]

In this letter he realised too that both his brothers Lionel and Herbert were home from South Africa, that he had missed writing to them: *I've seen so little of Bert.*

By May 16th however, Lugard had arrived and the guns too. *The guns go on tomorrow, but I have got a far better billet and go the day after. I go past them as I believe Chief Political Officer at the extreme front, beyond Boussa and behind the French. My duties are to watch the French, recruit Hausas and buy horses. I go by canoe with one Hausa sergeant for recruiting purposes.* A week later: *delayed by political developments, ready to start at a moment's notice for Yalma beyond Boussa. I march the whole way avoiding the river, with a white doctor, an escort of 10 mounted infantry and 3 months rations.* By the 29th his target was Kishi to the west not Yalma, since arguments with the French had eased. [73]

Despite the heat, the excitement and the stop-go changes, Alfred still enjoyed himself, *went across river to shoot guinea fowl for breakfast, met a leopard in the open and bagged it. I am sending the skin to Rowland Ward to send on to you.* In early June: *got a touch of fever, but got rid of it. Still keep my reputation as the fittest looking man in W. Africa. I feel it too.*

Alfred could also poke a bit of fun at his professional brother: *Nothing else to do but build houses. I shall soon rival Bert as an architect. They certainly let the water through but their style is unrivalled.*

Sketch of hut from Alfred's later letter of August 6th

Final orders to go were received on June 11th. His diary recorded the order: *Capt. Baker will now proceed to Kishi to recruit Hausas on the southern border of Borgu.* They crossed the river and set off the next day: *2 officers, 2 white NCOs, one black corporal, 32 carriers, with kit and a month's rations, 4 servants, 5 ponies. Rode a mare I paid £10 for and took Lucifer.*

33

Our route here lay through a forest entirely uninhabited and except for a couple of ruined villages up this end and a slave raiders' track used for sacking them, there is no sign of man for no one has ever been through it. Plenty of signs of other things though: elephant, lion, buffalo, antelope of all sorts... I got a couple of buck (oribi), most excellent venison. The water was dirty: the two things I longed for most were bread and water. The forest was not the least like the lower part near the coast, more like an English coppice.[74]

His diary picks up the thread at 11 am on June 16th: *I was riding last as rearguard. I saw the Shonga coolies (who as usual were right behind the others and had to be driven all the way) throw down their loads and rush away into the bush. Cpl Hutchins who was riding with them came galloping back. I asked him what was the matter and he did not know! I thought they were either deserting or had come on a lion (we had seen tracks not far off). I loaded my rifle (meaning to shoot in either case) and rode up. I soon found my mistake as arriving on the spot my mare and myself were attacked by a swarm of bees, who looked upon us as the cause of all the trouble. They attacked our heads going principally for the eyes, ears, nose and mouth. The mare in her agony threw herself down. My helmet came off and my foot got caught in the stirrup. The sole of my left boot being half off, it jammed in the stirrup so that my only way to get free was to tear off the sole. For 10 minutes we struggled, sometimes up, sometimes down. I twisted my knee but managed to keep the mare from bolting. This kept both hands busy and the bees held undisputed possession of my face. Eventually I got clear and put my coat over my head which was covered with blood. It took a long time to get clear of the bees though. I got to where the corporal and a few carriers were hiding in the bush, but the bees would not touch them, but followed me and my poor brute of a mare wherever we went. At last she stretched herself out as if she were dead. I did much the same, but to get to work to collect the carriers and drag them back to their loads. Eventually got them off, found my helmet, marched till 4.30 pm.*

Recovering from that he wrote to his mother a few days later to tell the tale, adding: *rather ignominious wasn't it? One could have had an adventure like that just as well in England as far as the bees were concerned, but I was expecting a lion.*

Reaching Kishi on June 19th he found it charming. There was a West Indian regiment and some Lagos constabulary. Later when some of them left, Alfred found himself in command of the station.

The French outpost seen across a stream at Kishi

The French have a post 200 yards away from us and we sit watching one another. We are much the strongest and hold the town though they came here first.

34

He had time now to sit and write, describing to his sister Bee, a dog lover, the adventures of his dog Lucifer who despite being gun-shy: *has done great swimming feats, three times swum the Niger and escaped the crocodiles. Once we started at daybreak up a river in canoes leaving Lucifer in camp. After half a mile we saw him following in mid stream, so we had to take him in. After crossing two rivers and miles of forest, at the first shot he bolts. I thought I was rid of him for good then, but on nearing camp, canoeing down the big river, who should we see but Lucifer swimming in mid stream to meet us.*[75]

Lucifer did not survive for long. Suffering from fever and a swollen head he died on June 30th. Alfred himself stayed fit, welcoming the cooler weather with regular storms and everything green and *apparently as healthy as Cobham but somehow horses, dogs and people get sick. I am getting a few recruits. We are teaching them to use a silver currency. They like silver 3[d] pieces for ornaments, but won't take half-crowns at all. However it is simpler than the barter system on the river.* There was a tour up the Benue River in prospect. *"Hope you are well as this leaves me", as Tommy says.*[76]

In one of his notebooks Alfred recorded the African recruits, each named with his trade, where he came from, the date and period signed on, usually 5 years, and whether he had passed a medical. Each received an advance of £1 and the "bringer", ie chief or trader who brought the man to Alfred, was recorded and paid a 5/- fee. There were 39 recruited between July 7 and August 4, of whom 10 were rejected on medical grounds. There was also an interpreter on his books paid 15/- on July 27.[77] But recruiting was *a delicate business as one is not allowed to kidnap slaves, yet we do not recognise slavery. All Hausas here are slaves, kept in chains now they tell us, as it has leaked out that I am enlisting Hausas as soldiers. Don't tell anyone about this for goodness sake.*

Then he got down to business: *Just had my weekly visit from the King. He was accompanied by a staff of 50 retainers, including his chiefs of warboys and the thunder-and-lightning maker. My retinue was all under my hat and seated on an inverted box. I dashed him a sovereign and a bottle of whiskey – rather excessive as I have tipped a king nine-pence – but I want to keep in with him as I am afraid I have been bagging some of his slaves. Not that £1 and a bottle represent the value of a slave as even a young girl the cheapest is worth a fiver. They are beginning to find out something about money, at times a three-penny piece is worth 5 shillings and a half-crown nothing.*[78]

He was also buying sheep as provisions for the troops still at Jebba, but: *three were killed during the night. Local hunters said 3 lions. I thought one leopard but tracks obliterated by carriers. Had a board on them of which I was president* – meaning he chaired an investigation – *and weight of evidence made it necessary to find it was the work of lions. Built a machan*[79] *and sat up from 9 to 5 am over the sheep, nothing came.* The next night: *sat up till 12, relieved by Swabey who left at 4.30, between then and 5 am sheep killed.* After that he did have some fever and had to neglect the problem. Worse: *had to shoot my mare, never really recovered from the attack of bees on the march, but died with symptoms of tsetse, a wasting sickness and hind legs much swollen. Up to the last fed well. Cost £10 originally.*

There is a note of realism in a letter apparently to Herbert at this time: *everyone takes enormous quantities of quinine. I think I take less than anybody. A lot of people start without taking it, but they very soon come to it after a couple of doses of fever.*

I am fitter than when I left England, but I have just had a couple of touches that make me believe in it. They come on for no apparent reason; that is the worst of it.[80]

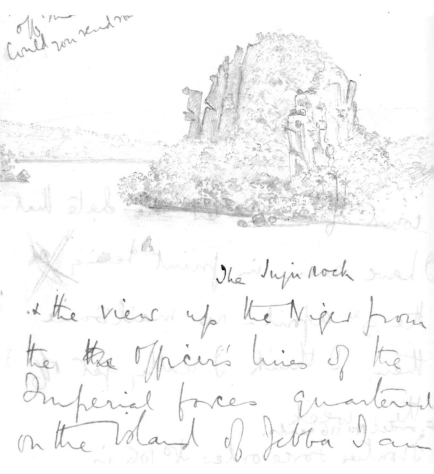

Recalled to Jebba, Alfred started back on August 13th with 20 carriers. He could obtain no horse so took a hammock: *lucky to get one. Don't care for the idea of being carried much. Found it no use as road much too bad.* It was a very different journey: *when we went up there was only one running stream to cross, on journey back forty. Had to make bridges, wade and swim but got through up to time in five days.* En route he bagged and recorded in his diary and game book: two oribi and a roan antelope, adding to his tally over 56 days at Kishi of 48 partridge, 21 green pigeon, 3 lesser bustard, two guineafowl, one each of plover, quail and hare.

Alfred often sketched the Juju rock on its island at Jebba

There were also *some lovely birds in the bush: multicoloured parrots, little things like sparrows bright scarlet, also light blue ones. I have taken over company today: 100 Hausas.* [81]

So whilst Alfred at last had his company of Hausa men and could do his real job of training them, there was a sequel to his days in The Sudan being played out. Alfred and others stuck in the tropics were well aware that there was more public esteem to be had up the Nile than up the Niger: *that Atbara campaign up the Nile is a pleasanter sort of show – 20 minutes – British heroes – back to lunch and champagne off the ice – Illustrated London News. I had a growl from a friend of mine a Captain in the Seaforth Highlanders, who instead of being there is alone up the Benue River buying cattle and ponies.*[82]

Back in Jebba, four days after taking over his company he was: *hard at work now drilling my Hausa company, the only one so far. I believe they are brave and faithful which is something, and can march all day when well.*[83] He soon acknowledged how quickly they learnt since there was no instruction in their own tongue.

Ostrich from August 6th letter

It was a bold move on his part as the wisdom of the time said that only Yorubas would make a fighting force and he was given the choice. However: *I commanded a guard of honour at the departure of Lugard and they were as smart as Guardsmen.* A later letter: *I believe there is a lot in them, especially the gentlemen among them who are the handsomest black men I have ever seen... We may very possibly have to fight their own brothers, but I believe they obey their own white man.*

His new role brought him confidence: *if I keep as fit as I have up to now, I almost think I shall take on for another year if I get a majority. I should bargain for six months at home next summer though...*

After recounting that he found 60 mosquitoes on himself one night in a tent, he wrote that *Koch was wrong about mosquitoes bringing fever, they do just the opposite, they take it out of you and certainly by that means spread it but not by stinging.*[84] He was still regularly out shooting. On September 3rd: *I stalked 8 teal in overflow from river, water to waist and long grass, and got right up to them, 25 yards... when an enormous crocodile put up his head ten yards from me. Had the sense to put up the teal and bag a right and left before returning to shore. Then had a shot at the crocodile and sent him off in a hurry, biggest I ever saw.*[85] *I shall not wade in there again.*

"The stalker stalked"

At the end of August Colonel Lugard left for England to confer with Chamberlain.[86] Lugard's deputy Col Fitzgerald went to Lagos, which meant that Alfred was temporarily in command of the battalion in Jebba and *had to send off a strong escort with Ultimatum to the Emir of Ilorin who has been playing the fool lately.*[87] Alfred chose Lt Dick Somerset to lead 50 men and by good fortune Somerset also left a diary (Ref 10). Somerset described a slow journey of about 60 miles as the rivers were high and they often needed to swim. Once there the Emir offered a cold shoulder so he camped outside Ilorin and constructed elaborate defences as much for his troops' morale as for any military purpose. Somerset deduced that the Emir wanted to fight but could not without agreement from other Emirs, some of whom were loyal to the British. In September Alfred wrote: *news from Ilorin promises war; don't believe it.* He was right, the Emir climbed down and Somerset returned.

October was the time to start exercises: *the first field day in Nigeria. Crossed over to North bank in canoes and joined Artillery. I was in command and did an attack on Armitage's irregulars, often in water up to one's waist.* There is more than just training in this as he had wind of something that would require them all to fight in earnest, though he could not say what or where, neither in his letters nor to his men. Would he at last see some action? He was keeping an eye on Ilorin, sending another detachment up river to prepare a new camp and settling companies of Nupés and Hausas on the opposite bank of the river. He was also running the camp with many of his staff sick. Major Morland (sketch right), senior to Alfred, *came down from Boussa, had been upset in rapids, lost all kit* and nearly drowned.[88] Though Alfred grumbled at being left all the work while more senior men were away or sick, *it is a great piece of luck as our first active operations are just coming off and I shall go in command. A DSO or Westminster Abbey. There are a lot of things in the wind, but I am sworn to secrecy.*[89] An officer, an NCO and 14 men had been killed in a skirmish *by an insignificant tribe.* He despatched an officer with 80 men and a maxim gun to restore order.[90]

The new huts were almost finished when at least one was demolished by a tornado. Whether he had dry accommodation is not clear, as in early October he was not as well as he usually claimed: *I have been suffering the tortures of the damned with neuralgia lately, following an ordinary little touch of the fever and it is far more unpleasant.* On October 27th however he organised a shooting match, Officers v NCOs, the officers winning easily. Alfred *shot last myself in dark. Made no miss.*[91]

He relayed in his next letter *a creditable story of 4 black soldiers of the WAFF in charge of an officer's baggage who were cut off in a march on the wrong side of a river and attacked by a large force. They refused to give it up and when fired on returned the fire, killed 15 men and 20 horses and got the baggage away. On another occasion 4 men swam the river to save another. One was taken by a crocodile but the others did what they went for. So I don't think they are bad chaps after all.*[92]

What action Alfred expected is a mystery. When war with the French was again in the rumour machine in early November, he dismissed it: *don't believe in slightest chance of war myself, but great anxiety in official circles.* On the 7th he wrote in his diary of a bad go of fever, followed by a bad night. He was up next morning however as there was musketry practice on the range, *but an awful worm. Still got fever.* Despite the fever: *we had to say whether we wanted to go home at the end of 12 months and whether we were willing to come out again. I said Yes to both. I met an old school fellow the other day and commanded the firing party at his funeral the day before yesterday. He was a civilian doctor named Rock, junior to me at school, whom I did not recognise in the bearded veteran I met here; a good fellow and the most uncomplaining patient.*[93]

Egga, November 19th, 1898, sketched while passing on the river

On November 11th, his fever gone, Alfred and two fellow officers went downstream two days to Lokoja on the *S S Empire*. No mention of who took over command at Jebba. *We were going back on the same steamer tomorrow but will have to stop a day or two as she had to go downstream to pull off another boat that has run aground.* They were away two weeks and that gave him time to sketch again.

The break brought Alfred encouragement, thanks to a communiqué: *I was mentioned in despatches last week, what for I don't know. "The Commissioner and Commandant desires to express his appreciation of the excellent work done by Major Cole, Major Morland, Capt Baker and Lieut Glossop in reconnaissance during their service in West Africa. The results of their work have been forwarded through the Secretary of State for the Colonies to the Intelligence Department." Hear! Hear! Loud cheers.*

Thanking his Mother for not missing a mail, he added: *hardly hear from anybody else. Most people look upon anyone who comes out here as a sort of lunatic they give up and hardly expect to see again... The fever does not bother me and I can always get rid of it with a couple of blankets being a free perspirer.*[94]

In Lokoja, to his delight: *I have been promised an excellent trip as soon as I get back, to march through the country with my company of 100 men, going to Kishi, Kyama and Boussa then back to Jebba if all is quiet. Just the sort of thing one wants.*

However, back up river at Jebba he took command of the Battalion there. On November 26th, he *sent "A" Company off by route march to Boussa under Welch with Legg, CS Barton, Cpls Matthews and Smith: 111 men, 120 carriers with 600 rounds a man.* The march was necessary because the canoes they had were *slow, bad and unseaworthy.* Alfred did not go himself because Col Fitzgerald his superior had returned to England and left him in command of the station. He did add to his diary for the 27th: *only three officers and six NCOs on parade this morning. Heard that two NCOs up river down with blackwater and Welchman sick en route for England. Seedy myself yesterday but all right today. Poole seedy too and Rock being dead leaves only one doctor. Bad time of year just after rain drying up.* But in contrast his letter home of the same day ends: *I am as fit as a fiddle, no neuralgia.*

Sketch from his diary
for November 27th

If he was disappointed at not going himself, he was soon busy: *I brought up our first lot of relief officers and NCOs. They are mostly sick already, although some are fresh from the Indian wars. They will soon find the happy medium between respecting and funking the climate.* Lifting his head a little: *I don't know what the future of this country is going to be, but they say there is a great opening for soldiers who can keep fit. The sooner the Government takes it over from the Niger Company the better for everybody. I wish they'd stop this uninteresting game of bluff with the French; it keeps us from getting on.* He is pleased with his training: *The soldiers are as disciplined as an Indian battalion. The band (fifes and drums) is getting on a great pace, can play four tunes with some skill. The buglers all learnt in 9 months. It would take me a lifetime to learn as much. I was four years over the Blue Bells of Scotland I remember.*[95]

The force was becoming seriously stretched: *Ordered by Commandant to find two officers and eight NCOs for 1st battalion and an OC* (officer to command) *for French frontier in Borgu. Don't see how I am to do it.*[96]

On December 7th his humour still shone: *Went up river to shoot with Booth and McClintock on Magi Island, opposite mouth of the Awon river. I knew the King of Magi having been there before when, in return for a dash of rice, I made him a handsome present of a sardine, which he shared with his Prime Minister (the latter got the tail).* They found nothing to shoot, but *the lions roared round one camp at night. I nearly trod on a small snake and shot the biggest cobra I ever saw (5 feet) and also got stung eight times by a scorpion that was in the knee of my breeches when I put them on. I had fever the first night, McClintock was seedy most of the time.*

Alfred wrote from Jebba on December 10th to his mother in England and to his brother Herbert in Cape Town. To Herbert he gave a longer view of *this stupid game of French bluff. I am off again this week as commandant of the French frontier in Southern and Eastern Borgu. Saki or Okuta will be my headquarters. We have made regular disciplined regiments who drill like the Guards. They have been through musketry. I like mine very much. They are just like dogs and would go to hell with one I believe.* Alfred saw no chance of trying them in a real battle, though more serious skirmishes were going on down river between the Niger Company and local tribes. He had orders to march on the 19th to Kyama, this being part of Chamberlain's continuing chessboard policy. *Carriers are the only means of transport on narrow bush tracks, thick forest on each side, ill adapted to a fighting formation in a hostile country with an enormous string of carriers. The Baribas of the country have always lived on highway robbery, never plant crops, but I don't think they would attack a white man. I have decided to come out here again and chance it, probably command a battalion for £1,000 a year or be second in command unless I make an ass of myself, which is always possible. A poor devil of a pauper must risk the climate for such good pay. The only thing I funk is going home a confirmed invalid.*[97]

A Merry Christmas

Alfred's story was almost at a close, those being his last two letters and his last drawing, sent as a Christmas card. His final diary entry was for December 12th: *Cole came back from S Borgu and took command.*[98] On the 16th he fell ill and died shortly after midnight on December 26th 1898 and was buried at Jebba later the same day. He was 34.

His parents would have heard first from Col Fitzgerald who was then in England. The Colonial Office had received the news by telegram. It was blackwater fever, a complication of malaria in which a parasite *Plasmodium falciparum* destroys red blood-cells, leading to black urine, fever and kidney failure. Blackwater fever, named by a doctor in Sierra Leone only 14 years earlier, killed many thousands in Africa at the time.

Dr Tichborne was with Alfred when he died and also Capt McClintock who had left Liverpool with him in February and had that month been shooting with him. There were many letters of condolence to his parents, all expressing his popularity and generosity. One comment that I was pleased to find was written not to his parents but in a diary, that of his colleague Dick Somerset: "Baker was one of the nicest chaps I had ever known, always cheery and jolly, good nature itself".[99]

Major Cole wrote from Jebba to say that he had sold Alfred's effects bar the trunk and its contents, his sword and gun. His mother was quick to write to Jebba to ask for details from those who were at his end, acknowledged by Dr Mayley and replied to by others. That must have been an agonising wait because mail was then taking at least a month each way. One letter of interest which was passed to the family was written by Alfred's colleague Lt Glossop to his brother Walter, another officer, recalling that only eight days before he died, Alfred had enjoyed a game of cricket, and "made all the runs and bowled everyone out". Perhaps not very strong opposition but at least Alfred could enjoy himself at such a late stage.

So ended a life of energy, fun and promise.

Two views of Capt A. W. Baker's grave at Jebba, Nigeria

It is good to know that memories of Alfred lived on for his parents, not just from his tin trunk, but also in letters from Jebba with photographs of his grave, recognition in his Battalion's newspaper, a Mention in Despatches and finally in a bronze memorial.

From early days I had been shown the bronze memorial high on the south side of the chancel of Cobham Church with an enamel regimental badge of the DLI, which is a bugle. From the trunk came both the petition with the signatures of many Cobham villagers for the memorial and the faculty[100] granted by the church to Alfred's father to install it (see back cover). Herbert chose the panel alongside for his own memorial and it is fitting that the two brothers, who were inseparable in early life, should be remembered together.

Within six weeks of Alfred's death, *The Bugle*, the DLI 2nd Battalion's weekly chronicle, published an obituary:

Poona, February 2nd, 1899:

The mail last Saturday brought the sad news of the death at Jebba on the 26th December last of Captain A W Baker, Durham Light Infantry, who was serving in the West Africa Frontier Field Force. The deceased who was 35 years of age was the son of T. H. Baker Esq of Cobham, Kent.

He joined the 2nd Battalion on 6th February 1884 at Gibraltar, was promoted Captain on the 19th April 1893 and transferred to the 1st Battalion, was re-transferred to the 2nd Battalion in September 1896, seconded from the Depot, Newcastle for special and active service under the Colonial Office on the 16th February 1898 and sailed for Lagos the same month. He served in The Sudan 1885-86 campaign under Sir F Stephenson, KCB with the regiment, Egyptian medal and Khedive Star.

Captain Baker was most universally popular and an exceedingly good all-round sportsman. He was educated at Tonbridge School succeeding in the Captaincy of both the cricket and the Rugby XV. At Sandhurst he was in the cricket XI and football XV and won many prizes at Athletic Sports, his most notable performance being a jump of 5 ft 8 inches which was a record at that time. For some years he was the mainstay of our Regimental cricket.

Glancing through the Regimental cricket book (which he started and of which the first part is all in his handwriting), we see that his first appearance for the Regiment was at Gibraltar on the 1st July 1884, when he made 17 in the first innings and 38 in the second. 1890 and 1892 were perhaps his most successful years in regimental cricket when he headed the averages with 56 and 31.3 runs respectively. Later he was a prominent player with the Northumberland County and Newcastle Garrison cricket clubs for whom he did great things in 1897.

He was a keen sportsman and an excellent draughtsman, as the Officers' Game Book will testify.

Our news form Jebba and Ibadan came from Major Fitzgerald and himself and only a few weeks ago a very cheery letter was received from him saying how well he was standing the climate. A favourite with everyone, his untimely death comes as a great shock to his numerous friends and the sincere sympathy of all of us is with his relations.

Finally in May 1899, Thomas Henry and Frances will have been comforted by the esteem surrounding their son when he was Mentioned in Despatches.

The following despatch has been received from the Secretary of State for the Colonies:

May 2, 1899

Sir, Mr Secretary Chamberlain has already brought to the notice of the Marquess of Lansdowne on the 22nd of February last the names of those officers and NCOs employed in the protected territories adjacent to the Gold Coast and Lagos and on the Niger, whose services in 1897 and the first 6 months of 1898 appeared to him to be deserving of special recognition. Further reports have now been received with regard to the organisation and work of the West African Frontier Force on the Niger during the first year of its existence and I am to ask that, the names of the following officers may be added to the list of those who have previously been mentioned for services in connection with this Force:

Captain (temp Major) W A Robinson, Royal Artillery,
Captain (temp Major) T L N Morland, King's Royal Rifle Corps,
Captain C G Blackader, Leicestershire Regt,
Captain F C Marsh, Royal West Kent Regt,
Capt P S Wilkinson, Northumberland Fusiliers,
Captain C F Goldie-Taubman, the King's Own Royal Lancaster Regt (since deceased),
Captain A W Baker, Durham Light Infantry (since deceased),
Lieutenant M H Toplin, Princess of Wales' Own (Yorkshire Regt),
Lieutenant B R M Glossop, 5th Dragoon Guards,
Lieutenant H Bryan, Lincolnshire Regt,
Lieutenant R H Buxton, Norfolk Regt,
Lieutenant C A Ker, R. A,
Lieutenant A B Molesworth, West India Regt,
Lieutenant C E J G O'Malley, 4th Bn Middlesex Regt.

I am, etc, R. L. Antrobus, The Under Secretary of State, War Office.

Alfred's well travelled tin trunk has once more come to rest. The letters, diaries, drawings and artefacts are now joined by this publication to create a picture of a soldier's life at the close of the Victorian era. The trunk lies in waiting for future generations to explore.

Acknowledgements

I acknowledge with thanks the many archives at national and local level which store and make available their treasures, especially that in Durham and its collection from the Durham Light Infantry. I must thank my wife Caroline for her patience and help in editing, Mike Spurgin for his photographs of Owletts and Cobham church and Hugh Andrew for his careful preparation of the maps.

References

1. T H Baker, *50 years of Cobham Cricket*, Wildish, Rochester 1899
2. Ronald Wingate, *Wingate of The Sudan*, 1955, page 88
3. M A Niguni, *A great trusteeship*, 1958, p 33
4. H E Raugh, *Victorians at War*, 2004
5. Memoirs of Field-Marshal Lord Grenfell, 1925, see pages 84 et seq.
6. S G P Ward, *Faithful; the story of the Durham Light Infantry,* 1962
7. W S Churchill, *History of the English Speaking peoples* Vol IV   page 369
8. W Gordon, *The Durham Light Infantry*, 1894, a tiny but informative booklet found in Alfred's trunk and given to every member of the Regiment, intended as its dedication reads "to be in reach of all ranks".
9. Margery Perham, *Lugard, the years of adventure 1858-1898*, 1956
10. Richard Somerset, *Diary of The Hon R F Somerset, Grenadier Guards, Adjutant the 2nd Bn the West African Field Force, Feb 1898 to Feb 1899.*
11. M McGregor, *Officers of the D. L. I. 1768 – 1968*

From Alfred's Army Book 119 C
Army Signalling Scribbling Book (Instructional Purposes Only).

Notes

[1] See my *The Samuel Bakers, Tradesmen of Kent*, 2008. Also *From Owletts to Iowa*, 2002

[2] Census of 1871, Civil parish of Cobham, page 31 from Ancestry.co.uk

[3] Alfred William was born on March 6th, 1864

[4] Alfred's notebook and diary D3 and *The Tonbridgian*, page 487, July 1882, also page 498.

[5] Royal Military Academy, Sandhurst Register, The National Archives (PRO) WO 151

[6] Alfred's bank book R2

[7] Alfred's letter AWB 1885 10 13 from aboard *SS Deccan*

[8] AWB 1885 10 25 from Abbasiyeh camp, near Cairo

[9] Quoted in Ref 4, H E Raugh's *Victorians at War* 2004, p 144

[10] Field Force State, Ginnis, 30 Dec 1885, report by Lt. Col Murray. PRO WO 110/10

[11] Telegram 38 from Cairo to War Office. PRO WO 110/10, page 13.

[12] AWB 1885 11 02 from Abbassiyeh camp, 1885 11 08 from Cairo

[13] AWB 1885 11 15 from Luxor

[14] AWB 1885 12 02 from Aswan and pages inserted in diary D3

[15] AWB 1885 12 06 from Tagoog Heights. His pay was 5s 3d a day plus Khedivial allowance 3s a day and 3s field allowance (bank book R2 and AWB 1885 12 02).

[16] AWB 1885 12 18 from Ambigola Wells. Alfred's preferred spelling of Koshay was Kosheh.

[17] Entry in Alfred's diary D1, dated 25 December 1885.

[18] AWB 1886 01 02 from Koyek, Sudan

[19] WO 110/10, page 26, items 62, 63, Kosheh 30, 31 December 1885, by Lt. Gen Stephenson

[20] AWB 1886 02 08 from Kosheh

[21] From DLI Archive's Digest of Services, 1885-1886, (D/DLI 2/2/14, pp.101-102). General Stephenson received the thanks of Parliament and the GCB for this action (ODNB 36277).

[22] AWB 1886 01 09 from Kosheh

[23] Ibid, AWB 1886 02 08

[24] There is a drawing and a plan of these forts at the PRO: WO 78 165

[25] AWB 1886 02 16

[26] Notebook D3. Also 10 of other species. AWB 1886 02 27 has the mule race and sketch of the forts

[27] ibid 1886 02 27, page dated March 6th.

[28] AWB 1886 03 24. His May 27 letter describes the sickness as enteric (typhoid).

[29] The sketch from Alfred's portfolio. A nuggar's capacity from the DLI's *The Bugle* 11 July 1895

[30] AWB 1886 04 15 and 04 17 and 04 22 to his sister Bee, all from Wady Halfa

[31] AWB 1886 05 01 from Tagoog Heights, Aswan

[32] AWB 1886 05 08 and 1886 05 27 from Tagoog Heights, the 27th letter had the sketch of Abu Simbel

[33] AWB 1886 06 01. He took 4 officers and 150 men, about 5% of the men of various regiments

[34] AWB 1886 06 11 from Ramleh

[35] AWB 1886 06 25 page 3 from Mt Troödos, Cyprus

[36] AWB 1886 06 01 from Aswan and 07 08 from Mt Troödos to his brother Ned

[37] Ibid, 1886 06 25 and 1886 07 11

[38] Cricket records mainly from AWB's notebook D3, also Tyne & Wear archives ref 3348

[39] Signalling at Poona 13 June 1891, musketry at Chunglagully 21 Dec. Riding at Mhow 13 June 1892.

[40] AWB 1890 01 29 from Poona

[41] AWB 1890 07 01 from Snowview, Dalhousie to his sister Bee

[42] AWB 1890 11 20 and 1891 01 17 from Quetta

[43] AWB 1890 10 00 also to Bee. The examinations would have been for the rank of Captain.

[44] Later General Sir Henry De Lisle, from Ref 11

[45] AWB 1891 02 09 from Quetta to Mrs Miller, which included the double sketch

[46] AWB 1891 09 26 with sketch from Changla Gali. Cricket records in D3.

[47] AWB 1891 12 22 from Sibi to Mrs Miller.

[48] Ibid AWB 1891 09 26, showing that he knew of this move 5 months ahead.

[49] My thanks for this photo to the DLI archive: item D/DLI 2/2/131 (88)

[50] AWB 1892 06 14. Cricket records in notebook D3 for 1893

[51] Alfred' promotion: *The Gazette* 18 April 1893. He listed dates and places (D3). He boarded the *S S Sutlej* on 2 June 1893.

[52] AWB 1893 11 19 from Buttevant

[53] AWB's *Pocket Game Register* from The E. C. Powder Company (R4). There was a woodcock shot at Owletts in November with Admiral Nicholson there.

[54] His cricket scores he kept in a notebook diary D3

[55] AWB 1895 02 19 from Tralee (this date is estimated from his Game book R4, possibly 1896 or 97)

[56] AWB 1895 05 21 from Ship Street barracks, Dublin

[57] Messrs Holt passbooks: R2 for 1884 to 1889 and R3 for August 1892 to August 1897

[58] Herbert Baker in Cape Town to his brother Ned, Feb 19, 1899

[59] AWB 1898 08 06 from Nigeria (see below)

[60] Ibid 1895 05 21. His last match in Ireland was for Military of Ireland v I Zingari on 16-17 August 1895, per invitation letter dated 30 June from F A Adam of the S. Lancashire Regt (loose leaf in D3).

[61] Written 14 January 1898 for *The Globe* newspaper, from PRO CO/445/1.

[62] McCallum in Lagos to Chamberlain, 4 August 1897

[63] PRO document CO 879 including the Telegram McCallum to Chamberlain 19 Sept 1897.

[64] AWB 1898 04 17 from R Niger north of Lokoja. His diary D11 recorded that the English-speaking Africans died too.

[65] AWB 1898 03 18 from Lokoja, River Niger

[66] AWB 1898 03 20 and 1898 03 31. Also R4 game record with others shooting with him

[67] AWB 1898 04 14

[68] AWB 1898 04 18 with sketch from his diary D11 for the same date

[69] Diary D11 entry for April 20th

[70] AWB 1898 04 27, 1898 05 07 and 05 15 from Jebba. As a captain he could expect to be commanding a Company of 100 Hausas.

[71] AWB 1898 05 08 from Jebba. The Maxim gun, an American invention later infamous in WW1, weighed about 60 kg and fired a 0.45 inch round, automatically reloading itself.

[72] Ibid 1898 05 15. It was a Lt Headlam of the Marines who was drowned.

[73] AWB 1898 05 17 from Jebba and 1898 05 25 finished 29 May

[74] AWB 1898 06 21 from Kishi and diary D11

[75] AWB 1898 06 21 to Bee and 06 23, both from Kishi. The outpost sketch from D11 diary, June 21st.

[76] AWB 1898 07 08 to his mother from Kishi

[77] Notebook D2, where he also laid out an order of march, copied from a document in PRO CO/445/2, in single file for 300 men plus their officers, guns, carriers, medical staff

[78] AWB 1898 07 19. This letter adds *I am earning £500 a year very cheaply.*

[79] Machan – a hunting blind. This from his diary for July 22nd.

[80] 2L12 980716 AWB, probably written to Herbert who passed it to Ned. Date not given, but estimated by comparing other letters with similar notepaper.

[81] Diary D11 for 22, 23 July and AWB 1898 08 12 from Kishi. The green pigeon *has a bright yellow breast, very good chop,* from AWB 1898 07 19. 1898 06 04 included this sketch of "Juju rock" at Jebba.

[82] AWB 1898 07 15 from Kishi, but I imagine Nigeria was more exciting to Alfred than Poona where the 2nd Battalion of the DLI was at the time.

[83] AWB 1898 08 23 from Jebba

[84] AWB 1898 09 01 and 10 19, both from Jebba. "A majority" was promotion to Major, in charge of three companies.

[85] Diary D11 entry for 3 Sept and AWB 1898 09 14 from Jebba

[86] Ref 9, page 706

[87] Diary D11 for 24 Sept and Oct 27. AWB 1898 11 08 from Jebba said that the Emir climbed down.

[88] Diary D11 for October 9th with sketch of Morland, who fought in WW1 and retired a General.

[89] AWB 1898 10 03 from Jebba

[90] Diary D11 for October 16 and AWB 1898 10 19

[91] AWB 1898 10 08 and Diary D11 for October 27.

[92] AWB 1898 10 25 from Jebba

[93] Diary D11 for November 2 and AWB 1898 11 08

[94] AWB 1898 11 14 from Lokoja and Diary D11 for November.

[95] Diary D11 for November 27th and AWB 1898 11 27 from Jebba

[96] Diary D11, also for November 17th

[97] AWB 1898 12 10a to Herbert from Jebba

[98] Diary D11 for December 7 and 12

[99] Ref 10, entry for December 26th. Somerset himself caught a chill on board ship to England and reached Liverpool but died four days later, on March 2nd, 1899

[100] Consistory Court of Rochester, 28 August 1901